Shadow Work Workbook
© Copyright 2023 by Grover Walton

TABLE OF CONTENTS

Dedicated to all my friends and to all the people
who gave me their help.
Thanks a lot
Thanks to all of you for your confidence
in my qualities and what I do.
Grover Walton

CHAPTER 1

UNDERSTANDING SHADOW WORK

What is Shadow Work?

Shadow work is a profound psychological journey that an individual undertakes to journey into their subconscious mind and confront the less pleasant aspects of their personality, often referred to as the "shadow self." This concept was first introduced by Swiss psychiatrist Carl Gustav Jung, who believed that integrating these hidden or suppressed aspects of ourselves is essential for achieving wholeness and self-acceptance.

In essence, shadow work is a self-reflective process of exploration and acceptance. It involves acknowledging and embracing the parts of ourselves that we'd rather not admit exist. These could be traits we've disowned, parts of ourselves we've deemed "bad" or "unacceptable" due to societal norms, personal beliefs, or traumatic experiences. They could also be latent abilities and strengths that we've yet to recognize or develop.

The "shadow self" is not necessarily negative. It merely comprises elements that we've pushed out of our conscious awareness. This could include positive attributes such as creativity, ambition, or assertiveness, which we may have suppressed due to fear, judgment, or the need to conform. By bringing these traits to light, we can accept, integrate, and utilize them in a healthy way, promoting personal growth and self-empowerment.

The process of shadow work can be challenging as it requires confronting, understanding and integrating aspects of ourselves that we've denied or ignored. However, it's also rewarding as it leads to increased self-awareness, self-acceptance, authenticity, personal power, and emotional freedom. By acknowledging and integrating our shadow self, we become more compassionate towards ourselves and others, as we understand that everyone encompasses a spectrum of traits, emotions, and potentialities.

Shadow work is not a one-time task but an ongoing process of self-discovery and self-improvement. It's not about eliminating our "shadow" or striving for some ideal of perfection. Rather, it's about acknowledging all parts of ourselves, understanding their origins, their impact on our lives, and then taking conscious control over them, so they no longer control us subconsciously.

A key aspect of shadow work is understanding that our perception of the world around us, including our interactions with others, is significantly influenced by our shadow self. For instance, certain traits or behaviors in others that strongly trigger or annoy us can point to disowned parts of ourselves. By recognizing these "projections," we can uncover and integrate these hidden aspects, leading to healthier and more harmonious relationships.

Another important aspect of shadow work is dream analysis. According to Jung, our dreams often contain symbolic representations of our shadow self. By interpreting these symbols, we can gain insights into our subconscious mind and further our shadow work journey.

In essence, shadow work is a journey towards self-acceptance and wholeness. It's about embracing all aspects of ourselves—our strengths and weaknesses, our virtues and vices, our potentialities and limitations. It's about understanding that we are multifaceted beings and that every aspect of us has a purpose and a role in our personal growth and self-realization. By undertaking this journey, we not only improve our relationship with ourselves but also our relationships with others, as we become more understanding, tolerant, and compassionate.

The Importance of Shadow Work in Personal Development

Delving into the unseen parts of ourselves is a crucial component of personal development. Often, the aspects of ourselves we keep hidden or suppressed are the very elements that hold us back from achieving our full potential. Unraveling these hidden parts of our psyche allows us to gain a deeper understanding of ourselves, our motivations, and our behaviors, helping us grow and develop in significant ways.

One of the key benefits of shadow work is increased self-awareness. By confronting and acknowledging our shadow self, we become more aware of our thoughts, emotions, and behaviors and why we react the way we do in certain situations. This awareness is the first step towards change, enabling us to make conscious decisions rather than just reacting based on subconscious patterns.

Another benefit is improved relationships. Frequently, the traits we deny in ourselves, we project onto others. For example, if we have suppressed our anger, we might be overly sensitive to anger in others. Recognizing and integrating these projections can help us respond more appropriately and constructively in our interactions with others, leading to healthier and more satisfying relationships.

Moreover, shadow work can lead to increased authenticity. By embracing all parts of ourselves, including the ones we'd rather hide or deny, we become more authentic in our interactions with others. We no longer feel the need to wear masks or pretend to be someone we're not. This authenticity can improve our relationships and increase our overall satisfaction with life.

Shadow work can also enhance our resilience. By acknowledging and dealing with our painful emotions and experiences, rather than suppressing or avoiding them, we become more resilient in the face of adversity. Instead of being derailed by difficult emotions or situations, we can accept them as part of life and deal with them in a healthy way.

Furthermore, shadow work can unleash our potential. Often, our shadow self contains untapped skills, abilities, and passions. By bringing these into conscious awareness, we can utilize them to enrich our lives and achieve our goals.

Finally, shadow work can lead to greater self-acceptance and self-compassion. By acknowledging and accepting all parts of ourselves, we cultivate a more compassionate attitude towards ourselves. We recognize that everyone has strengths and weaknesses, virtues and vices, and we become kinder and more forgiving towards ourselves.

The journey into our shadow is not an easy one. It requires courage, honesty, and commitment. It can bring up painful emotions and memories. But it is also a journey of discovery, healing, and transformation. As we integrate our shadow self, we become more whole, more authentically ourselves. We become better able to navigate the challenges of life, to form meaningful relationships, and to realize our full potential. Shadow work, therefore, is a vital part of personal development, a path that leads to greater self-awareness, self-understanding, and personal growth.

Identifying the Shadow Self

A crucial step on the journey of personal growth is recognizing and understanding the shadow self. This hidden aspect of our personality harbors traits, impulses, and emotions that, for various reasons, we've chosen to suppress or deny. Identifying these elements can be challenging, as they often exist outside our conscious awareness. However, a few practical strategies can aid in this process of discovery and acceptance.

One of the primary methods to identify the shadow self is through introspection and self-reflection. Paying attention to patterns in our thoughts, emotions, and behaviors can reveal aspects of our shadow self. For instance, habitual negative thought patterns or recurring emotional reactions may point to underlying shadow elements. Keeping a journal can be a useful tool in this process, allowing for detailed tracking and analysis of these patterns.

Dream analysis can also provide valuable insights into our shadow self. Our dreams often reflect our subconscious mind, and by interpreting recurring symbols or themes, we can uncover aspects of our shadow self. This process, however, often requires a good understanding of dream symbolism or the assistance of a professional.

Another powerful method for identifying the shadow self is projection. When we strongly dislike or get irritated by certain qualities in others, it often indicates that we are projecting our shadow self onto them. These are typically traits that we've disowned in ourselves. By identifying and understanding these projections, we can uncover the elements of our shadow self.

However, it's important to remember that the goal of identifying the shadow self is not to eliminate these traits or emotions but to accept and integrate them. This doesn't mean acting out these traits but rather acknowledging them and understanding their origins and impact on our lives.

While identifying the shadow self can be an uncomfortable process, it is also incredibly liberating. It allows us to take control of our lives, improve our relationships, and grow as individuals. It enables us to understand and change behaviors that may have been sabotaging our happiness and success. It brings us closer to authenticity, self-acceptance, and wholeness.

Shadow work is not a quick or easy process, and it often requires courage and persistence. However, the rewards are well worth the effort. By making the unconscious conscious, we can free ourselves from the chains of past traumas and negative patterns, and step into our true, authentic selves.

As we learn to embrace our shadow, we also learn to embrace our light – our strengths, our talents, our potential. We develop a deeper understanding of who we truly are, and we gain the freedom to express ourselves fully and authentically. In essence, identifying the shadow self is a journey of self-discovery, a journey towards wholeness and authenticity. It is a journey that can transform not only our relationship with ourselves but also our relationship with the world around us.

Common Misconceptions About Shadow Work

Diving into the realm of shadow work can be an enlightening experience, but it's also an area that's often misunderstood. Several misconceptions can cloud our understanding and potentially hinder our progress on this transformative journey. Addressing these misconceptions is vital to approach shadow work with clarity and purpose.

One common misconception is that shadow work is purely negative, focusing only on the darker aspects of our personality. While it's true that shadow work involves uncovering and embracing our suppressed or denied traits, it's essential to note that the 'shadow self' isn't inherently bad. It can contain undiscovered strengths, talents, and positive attributes. The goal of shadow work isn't to dispel the shadow but to acknowledge, understand, and integrate it.

Another misconception is that shadow work encourages self-criticism or self-blame. This couldn't be further from the truth. Shadow work is about self-acceptance and compassion. It's about understanding that everyone has a shadow self and that acknowledging this is part of our human experience. It's not about blaming ourselves for our flaws but understanding these aspects to foster growth and healing.

A third misconception is that shadow work is a quick fix for personal issues. Shadow work is a profound, ongoing process. It's not about instant gratification but deep, lasting transformation. It requires patience, commitment, and time. One can't rush the process or expect immediate results.

Additionally, many people mistakenly believe that shadow work should always be done alone. While personal reflection is a significant part of the process, guidance from a skilled therapist, counselor, or coach can be incredibly beneficial. Having external support can provide a fresh perspective, help navigate challenging emotions, and ensure the process is safe and effective.

Lastly, some people may think that once they've done shadow work, they're finished. However, shadow work is a lifelong journey. As we grow and evolve, new layers of our shadow self may surface, requiring further exploration and integration.

Contrary to these misconceptions, shadow work is not a negative, blame-centric, quick, solitary, or one-time process. It's a positive journey towards self-understanding, compassion, patience, and lifelong learning. It's about integrating all aspects of our being, the light, and the shadow, to become the most authentic version of ourselves.

While shadow work can be challenging, it is also incredibly rewarding. It can lead to a deeper understanding of ourselves, greater self-acceptance, improved relationships, and a richer, more authentic life. It can liberate us from the chains of our past and empower us to live fully in the present. So, as you embark on this journey, remember to approach it with an open mind, compassion, patience, and a willingness to embrace all that you are.

CHAPTER 2

THE JOURNEY TO SELF-DISCOVERY

Identifying Your Emotional Triggers

The process of identifying emotional triggers is a critical aspect of shadow work. Emotional triggers are situations, words, emotions, or experiences that provoke an intense emotional reaction within us. They often stem from past traumas or unresolved issues, and they can cause us to react in ways that are disproportionate to the actual situation at hand.

The first step in identifying your emotional triggers is to practice mindfulness. This means paying attention to your thoughts, feelings, and reactions in different situations. When you notice a strong emotional response, take a moment to pause and reflect on what might have triggered it. You might find it helpful to keep a journal where you can note down these experiences and your reactions to them.

Some triggers can be quite obvious. For example, if you had a difficult relationship with a parent, you might find that you get triggered by behaviors in others that remind you of that parent. Other triggers might be less obvious and require some deeper introspection. They might be linked to experiences that you've forgotten or suppressed, or they might be associated with certain beliefs about yourself or the world that you've adopted.

Next, it's important to explore the origin of these triggers. Understanding why certain things trigger you can help you to process these emotions and reduce their impact on your life. This might involve reflecting on your past and considering any traumatic events or difficult experiences that might have contributed to these triggers.

Once you've identified a potential trigger, you can start to work on desensitizing yourself to it. This might involve gradually exposing yourself to the trigger in a safe and controlled way while practicing calming techniques. Over time, this can help to lessen your emotional reaction to the trigger.

It's important to remember that this process can be difficult and that it's okay to seek help. A therapist or counselor can provide guidance and support as you work through your triggers and can help you to develop effective coping strategies.

Emotional triggers can feel like obstacles on your path to personal growth, but they can also be seen as signposts pointing towards areas of your life that need healing. By identifying and working through your triggers, you can free yourself from past traumas, reduce the control that these triggers have over your life, and move towards greater emotional freedom and wellbeing.

Uncovering your emotional triggers is not about blaming others for your reactions. It's about claiming responsibility for your emotional well-being. It's about understanding that while you can't control what happens to you, you can control how you respond. And most importantly, it's about recognizing that you have the power to heal and transform your life.

Understanding Your Emotional Responses

Understanding your emotional responses is a key component in personal growth and self-improvement. Emotions are our internal barometer, signaling what's happening within us in response to external or internal stimuli. They can serve as valuable indicators, shedding light on our needs, values, and experiences.

To begin understanding your emotional responses, it's essential to develop emotional awareness. This involves recognizing when you're experiencing an emotion, being able to name that emotion, and understanding why you're feeling it. It may seem simple, but many people find it challenging, particularly if they've grown up in environments where emotional expression was discouraged.

A practical way to enhance emotional awareness is by practicing mindfulness, a form of meditation where you focus on being intensely aware of what you're sensing and feeling in the moment, without interpretation or judgment. When an emotion arises, instead of immediately reacting, take a moment to observe it. What is the emotion? Where do you feel it in your body? What thoughts are associated with it?

Journaling can also be a powerful tool in understanding your emotional responses. Writing about your emotions can help you to express and understand them more clearly. It can help you to identify patterns in your emotional responses and explore possible triggers.

Once you've identified an emotion, it's important to explore it further. Ask yourself, "What is this emotion trying to tell me?" For instance, fear might be warning you about potential danger or risk, while anger might be signaling that your boundaries have been crossed.

It's also vital to understand that each emotion serves a function and has value. Society often labels emotions as "good" or "bad," but all emotions are important. For instance, sadness can signal a need for comfort and healing, while joy can inspire us to pursue certain activities or relationships.

Another crucial part of understanding your emotional responses is accepting them. Many people judge themselves for their emotions, particularly those seen as negative. However, it's important to remember that all emotions are a normal part of the human experience and it's okay to feel them.

Understanding your emotional responses is not a process that happens overnight. It requires patience, practice, and compassion towards oneself. However, the benefits are worth it. It can lead to greater self-awareness, improved emotional regulation, better decision-making, and healthier relationships.

Finally, remember that it's okay to seek help if you're struggling to understand your emotional responses. Therapists and counselors are trained to help you navigate your emotional landscape and can provide tools and strategies to assist in your journey. The journey to understanding your emotional responses is a journey to understanding yourself. And with this understanding comes the power and freedom to navigate your life with more self-awareness, compassion, and authenticity.

The Role of the Subconscious Mind

Delving into the depths of the human mind, we encounter the subconscious, a powerful layer that greatly influences our thoughts, emotions, and behaviors. This 'undercurrent' is always active, storing memories, experiences, and beliefs that shape our perception of reality and guide our actions. Understanding the role of the subconscious mind can provide significant insights into our personal development journey.

The subconscious mind is like a massive memory bank. Its capacity is virtually unlimited and it permanently stores everything that ever happens to you. It holds your life experiences, your beliefs, your memories, your skills, all situations you've been through, and all images you've ever seen.

One of the primary roles of the subconscious mind is to filter reality: it seeks to validate what matches your existing beliefs and dismisses anything that doesn't. This automatic filtering process helps us navigate the world but can also limit our perspective, trapping us in conditioned ways of thinking and reacting.

The subconscious mind also influences our bodily functions. Think about it: you don't have to consciously think about breathing, your heart beating, or your digestive system working. All of these processes are managed by the subconscious mind.

Another crucial role of the subconscious mind lies in its influence over our emotional responses and behavior patterns. Most of our emotional reactions and automatic behaviors originate from the subconscious mind. Our habits, phobias, fears, and automatic responses are all stored in the subconscious, making it the direct source of our behavioral patterns.

The subconscious mind is also the realm of the imagination. It's where our dreams and daydreams come from. It's where we visualize scenarios and outcomes, which is a powerful tool in manifesting our goals and desires.

Understanding the role of the subconscious mind allows us to harness its power. We can reprogram the subconscious mind with positive beliefs and habits through techniques such as affirmations, visualization, hypnosis, and various forms of therapy.

While the subconscious mind might seem like a mysterious entity, it's essentially a data-bank for everything, which is not in your conscious mind. It's the storage space for all your past experiences, your deep-seated beliefs, your memories, your skills, your previous life experiences. It's the source of your creativity and your spiritual life. Understanding the subconscious mind opens up new possibilities for personal growth and self-improvement.

The subconscious mind is a powerful ally. When we understand its role and learn to work with it, we can unlock our potential, overcome challenges, and create meaningful change in our lives. It's a journey of discovery, a journey towards understanding ourselves, a journey of personal growth and transformation. And it's a journey that can lead to greater self-awareness, empowerment, and fulfillment.

Techniques for Exploring Your Inner Self

Unlocking your inner self can be akin to embarking on a great adventure. It is an exploration of your inner depths, a journey into the unseen landscapes of your emotions, beliefs, desires, and dreams. It offers a wealth of insights and discoveries that can fuel personal growth. Several techniques can aid in this exploration and provide you with valuable self-knowledge.

Meditation is one of the most potent tools for inner exploration. By quieting the chatter of the conscious mind, meditation allows us to tune into our inner world. It encourages self-observation, fosters inner peace, and can illuminate our deepest desires and fears. Starting with simple mindfulness meditation—focusing on your breath or bodily sensations—can be a practical first step.

Journaling is another powerful technique for self-exploration. Writing about your thoughts, feelings, and experiences can lead to profound self-discoveries. It allows you to express yourself freely, without judgment, and can reveal patterns, trigger points, and deep-seated beliefs that you might not have noticed otherwise.

Practicing introspection is also critical. This involves consciously exploring your thoughts, emotions, and beliefs. It's about asking yourself thought-provoking questions, like "Why do I react this way?" or "What beliefs are driving this thought?" Introspection can help you understand your motivations, reactions, and behaviors at a deeper level.

Artistic expression can be a beautiful and therapeutic way to explore your inner self. Whether it's painting, writing poetry, playing an instrument, or dancing, creative activities can help you express and understand your emotions, experiences, and perspectives in unique ways.

Finally, seeking professional guidance can be invaluable. Therapists and counselors are trained to help you navigate your inner world. They can provide tools, techniques, and perspectives that can aid your self-exploration journey and help you overcome any barriers you might encounter along the way.

These techniques are only starting points in your exploration of the inner self. Everyone's journey is unique, and what works for one person might not work for another. It's important to find the methods that resonate with you and align with your personal needs and circumstances.

In the process of exploring your inner self, it's crucial to cultivate an attitude of openness, curiosity, and self-compassion. There will likely be surprises, challenges, and moments of discomfort. But there can also be moments of profound insight, self-understanding, and transformation. Each step you take on this journey is a step towards greater self-awareness, authenticity, and personal growth.

Exploring your inner self isn't a destination but a journey. It's a lifelong adventure of self-discovery, self-understanding, and self-transformation. And it's a journey that has the potential to enrich your life in countless ways, bringing greater depth, meaning, authenticity, and fulfillment. It's a journey well worth embarking on.

CHAPTER 3

TOOLS FOR TRANSFORMATION

The Power of Thoughts and Beliefs

Akin to a rudder guiding a ship, our thoughts and beliefs steer the course of our lives. They influence our attitudes, emotions, behaviors, and ultimately, our experiences. Understanding the power of thoughts and beliefs is an essential aspect of personal growth and transformation.

Every thought we have can be seen as a seed, with the potential to grow into a belief. When we repeatedly think the same thought, it can solidify into a belief and become a part of our worldview. These beliefs then influence how we interpret our experiences, how we react, and how we make decisions.

For instance, if you hold the belief that you're not good enough, it can affect your confidence, your willingness to take risks, and your ability to form healthy relationships. Conversely, if you believe that you're capable and deserving, it can fuel your motivation, boost your resilience, and enhance your overall well-being.

While beliefs are powerful, it's vital to remember that they're not always accurate. Many of our beliefs are formed in childhood, based on our interpretation of experiences rather than objective facts. Over time, these beliefs can become ingrained, even if they no longer serve us or align with our current reality.

The good news is, beliefs are not set in stone. They can be changed. Cognitive restructuring, a type of cognitive-behavioral therapy, is one method that can help. It involves identifying and challenging irrational or harmful beliefs and replacing them with healthier, more balanced ones.

Mindfulness and meditation can also be effective in transforming thoughts and beliefs. By cultivating awareness of our thoughts, we can choose not to engage with those that are negative or unhelpful. Over time, this can change the pattern of our thinking and consequently, our beliefs.

Affirmations are another tool for reshaping our beliefs. Regularly repeating positive, empowering statements can help to reprogram our belief system and foster a more positive mindset.

Lastly, professional therapy or counseling can provide invaluable support in understanding and reshaping your belief system. Therapists are trained to help you navigate your thoughts and beliefs and can provide tools and strategies to assist in your journey.

Thoughts and beliefs are powerful forces, but they're also within your control. By understanding the power of thoughts and beliefs, and learning how to harness this power, you can guide the course of your life towards greater happiness, fulfillment, and personal growth.

The journey of exploring and transforming your thoughts and beliefs is an empowering process. It's about reclaiming your power, fostering self-awareness, and creating a life that aligns with your true desires and values. It's a journey that can lead to profound personal growth and a profound sense of freedom and authenticity.

How to Change Your Limited Beliefs

Altering limited beliefs is akin to releasing weights that have been holding you down. These beliefs, often formed in our early life, can constrict our potential and keep us stuck in patterns that don't serve our growth. By changing these beliefs, we can free ourselves and open up new possibilities for our lives.

To begin altering your limited beliefs, you first need to identify them. This might involve self-reflection, journaling, or working with a therapist or coach. Look for patterns in your thoughts or behaviors that might indicate underlying beliefs. For instance, if you often find yourself avoiding new challenges, you might hold a belief that you're not capable or competent.

Once you've identified a limited belief, seek to understand its origin. Understanding where a belief comes from can help you see it for what it is: a thought that you've accepted as truth, often based on past experiences rather than current reality.

Next, challenge the belief. Ask yourself, "Is this belief really true?" "Does it apply to me now, in my current situation?" "Does it serve my growth and happiness?" It can be helpful to gather evidence that contradicts the belief. For example, if you believe you're not good enough, list your accomplishments and strengths.

After challenging your limited belief, replace it with a new, empowering belief. This should be a belief that supports your growth, happiness, and overall well-being. For instance, you might replace "I'm not good enough" with "I am capable and deserving of success."

Affirmations can be a powerful tool in this process. Regularly repeating your new belief can help to reprogram your mind and solidify the belief.

Visualization can also aid in changing limited beliefs. Imagine yourself living with your new belief. How would you think, act, or feel differently? Visualization can help make the new belief feel more real and achievable.

Changing limited beliefs takes time and practice. Be patient with yourself and celebrate your progress along the way.

Lastly, remember that it's okay to seek help. Changing limited beliefs can be challenging, and having support can make the process easier. A therapist or coach can provide guidance, encouragement, and tools to aid in your journey.

The process of changing limited beliefs is a journey of self-liberation. It's about freeing yourself from outdated, restrictive mindsets and embracing beliefs that uplift you, empower you, and support your growth. And it's a journey that can lead to greater self-confidence, fulfillment, and overall well-being. It's a journey of self-discovery and transformation, a journey towards a more authentic and empowered life.

The Role of Meditation in Shadow Work

The journey into shadow work, a process of exploring and integrating the less acknowledged parts of our selves, can be greatly enhanced by the practice of meditation. As a tool for fostering self-awareness, mindfulness, and compassion, meditation plays a significant role in successfully navigating this transformative journey.

Meditation provides a space for stillness and reflection, which are essential in shadow work. It allows us to slow down, turn inward, and observe our thoughts and feelings without judgment. This mindful observation can reveal patterns, trigger points, and shadow aspects that might otherwise remain hidden under the hustle and bustle of everyday life.

Meditation also fosters a non-judgmental attitude, which is crucial in shadow work. It teaches us to observe our thoughts, feelings, and experiences without labeling them as 'good' or 'bad'. This non-judgmental awareness can make it easier for us to acknowledge and accept our shadow aspects.

Another indispensable quality meditation cultivates is compassion, both for ourselves and others. Shadow work often brings us face-to-face with parts of ourselves we may find difficult or uncomfortable. Cultivating compassion through meditation can help us approach these aspects with kindness and understanding, rather than rejection or criticism.

Meditation also helps in grounding and centering oneself, which can be particularly beneficial during the often intense process of shadow work. It can provide a sense of stability and calm amidst the storm, helping us navigate the journey with grace and resilience.

There are various forms of meditation that can be beneficial in shadow work. Mindfulness meditation is one of the most effective, as it encourages present-moment awareness and acceptance. Loving-kindness meditation can also be beneficial, as it fosters a sense of compassion and understanding.

It's important to remember that meditation is a practice, and like any other skill, it takes time and consistency to reap its benefits. Start with short sessions and gradually increase the duration as your comfort and concentration improve.

Finally, consider seeking guidance if you're new to meditation or find it challenging. Many resources are available, from guided meditations and apps to classes and workshops. A skilled teacher can provide valuable guidance and support as you incorporate meditation into your shadow work journey.

Incorporating meditation into your shadow work practice can enrich the process significantly. It can provide the space, awareness, and compassion necessary to delve into your inner world and embrace all aspects of yourself. It's a journey of self-discovery, self-acceptance, and ultimately, self-transformation.

Meditation is not just a tool for relaxation or stress relief. It's a powerful practice that can illuminate your inner landscape, foster deep self-understanding, and catalyze profound personal growth. It's a journey into the heart of who you are, a journey of awakening, and a journey towards a more authentic, integrated, and fulfilled life.

The Mirror Technique: A Guide

As a method for self-improvement and personal growth, the Mirror Technique is a powerful tool. This practice involves standing in front of a mirror and speaking directly to your reflection, affirming your worth, acknowledging your progress, and addressing areas for growth. This guide will outline how to effectively use the Mirror Technique to foster self-awareness and enhance personal development.

To start with the Mirror Technique, find a quiet and private space where you can comfortably stand in front of a mirror. It's important to be in a space where you feel safe and won't be interrupted. Take a few moments to ground yourself, taking deep, calming breaths to center your mind and body.

Begin by looking directly into your eyes in the mirror. This can feel uncomfortable at first, but it's a key part of the process. Eye contact with yourself fosters a deep connection with your inner self.

Next, start speaking to your reflection. You might start with affirmations, positive statements about yourself and your abilities. For example, you might say, "I am capable," "I am worthy," or "I am growing stronger every day." Speak with conviction, even if you don't fully believe the words at first.

In addition to affirmations, you can use the Mirror Technique to address your challenges. Speak openly about what you're struggling with and express your commitment to overcome these obstacles. You might say, "I acknowledge my fear, but I won't let it control me," or "I am committed to improving my patience."

Throughout this process, observe your emotions without judgment. If you feel resistance, discomfort, or emotion welling up, allow it. These reactions can provide valuable insights into your subconscious beliefs and emotional state.

The Mirror Technique is not a one-time activity; it's a practice. Regularly dedicating time to this technique can lead to profound shifts in your self-perception and confidence.

While the Mirror Technique can be a powerful tool for personal growth, it's important to approach it with patience and self-compassion. Change takes time, and it's okay to feel uncomfortable or resistant in the process.

Finally, remember that it's okay to seek support. If you're finding the Mirror Technique particularly challenging or confronting deep-seated beliefs and emotions, consider seeking the support of a therapist or counselor. They can provide guidance and tools to help navigate your journey of self-discovery and growth.

The Mirror Technique is more than a practice; it's a journey towards self-love, self-acceptance, and self-improvement. It's about facing yourself with honesty, embracing your strengths, acknowledging your weaknesses, and committing to personal growth. It's a journey towards a more confident, authentic, and self-aware you. And it's a journey that can transform your relationship with yourself, fostering greater self-compassion, self-belief, and self-respect.

The 3-2-1 Method: A Comprehensive Guide

In the world of personal development and self-improvement, the 3-2-1 Method stands as an effective strategy for fostering awareness, growth, and transformation. This method involves three simple steps: identifying three positive aspects, two areas for improvement, and one action step. This comprehensive guide will explore how to implement the 3-2-1 Method in your daily life.

Let's begin with the first step: identifying three positives. These could be traits you appreciate about yourself, accomplishments you've achieved, or positive habits you've cultivated. The key is to acknowledge and celebrate these aspects of yourself. This step fosters gratitude and positivity, enhancing your self-perception and boosting your confidence.

Next, identify two areas for improvement. These could be habits you want to change, skills you want to develop, or attitudes you want to shift. It's important to approach this step with self-compassion and understanding, seeing it as an opportunity for growth rather than a criticism.

The final step is to identify one action step that you can take towards improvement. This could be a new habit to cultivate, a negative pattern to break, or a personal goal to pursue. The key is to make this action step specific, achievable, and relevant to your areas for improvement.

Implementing the 3-2-1 Method into your daily routine can be straightforward. You might choose to do it in the morning to set a positive tone for your day, or in the evening as a form of reflection. You could write down your 3-2-1 in a journal, discuss them with a supportive friend or partner, or simply go over them in your mind.

The beauty of the 3-2-1 Method lies in its simplicity and flexibility. It can be tailored to your individual needs and goals, and can be used to support various aspects of personal growth, from self-esteem and mindfulness to productivity and goal-setting.

Personal growth is a journey, not a destination. The 3-2-1 Method is a tool that can guide you on this journey, fostering self-awareness, self-improvement, and positive change. But it's not a magic solution. It requires consistency, honesty, and self-compassion.

Incorporating the 3-2-1 Method into your daily routine is a commitment to yourself and your personal growth. It's an affirmation of your worthiness and potential. And it's a journey towards a more self-aware, empowered, and fulfilled you.

Remember, the 3-2-1 Method is not just a technique but a philosophy of continuous self-improvement. It's about acknowledging your strengths, recognizing your potential for growth, and taking concrete steps towards your desired changes. It's a journey of self-discovery, self-improvement, and transformation, a journey towards a more authentic, self-aware, and fulfilled life.

CHAPTER 4

HEALING YOUR INNER WOUNDS

Understanding and Overcoming Trauma

The journey of understanding and overcoming trauma can be likened to traversing a challenging but ultimately rewarding mountain path. It involves facing painful experiences, fostering self-awareness, and cultivating resilience and healing. This journey is unique for each individual, but various strategies can provide support along the way.

Trauma refers to deeply distressing or disturbing experiences that can have long-lasting impacts on our mental, emotional, and physical well-being. It can stem from a range of events, including physical or emotional abuse, accidents, natural disasters, or significant losses. The effects of trauma can manifest in various ways, such as anxiety, depression, flashbacks, physical symptoms, or changes in behavior or relationships.

Understanding trauma is the first step towards overcoming it. This involves acknowledging the traumatic event and recognizing its impact on your life. It's important to remember that everyone's experience with trauma is unique and there's no 'right' or 'wrong' way to respond to such events.

One of the key strategies in overcoming trauma is seeking professional support. Therapists and counselors trained in trauma-informed care can provide valuable tools and techniques to help you navigate your healing journey. They can help you explore and make sense of your experiences, develop coping mechanisms, and work towards recovery.

Self-care is another crucial component of overcoming trauma. This might involve regular exercise, a balanced diet, sufficient sleep, relaxation techniques, and activities you enjoy. These practices can help manage stress, boost your mood, and foster overall well-being.

Mindfulness and meditation can also be beneficial in dealing with trauma. They can help you stay present and centered, reduce stress and anxiety, and cultivate a sense of inner peace.

Support from loved ones can also be invaluable in overcoming trauma. Sharing your experiences with trustworthy friends or family members can provide emotional support, reduce feelings of isolation, and foster a sense of connection.

Lastly, remember that it's okay to take your time. Healing from trauma is not a linear process, and it's okay to have ups and downs. Be patient with yourself and celebrate your progress along the way.

Understanding and overcoming trauma is a journey of healing and resilience. It's about facing your past, nurturing your present, and building a future that aligns with your strength and potential. It's a journey that can lead to profound personal growth and a deeper understanding of yourself and your capacity for resilience.

Overcoming trauma is more than just recovery—it's about transformation. It's about rising from the ashes, reassessing your life, and using the experience as a catalyst for growth and change. It's a journey that can lead to a newfound strength, a deeper understanding of oneself, and a more enriched and fulfilling life.

Exploring Your Inner Child

Embarking on the journey of exploring your inner child can be a transformative experience. This exploration involves connecting with the child you once were, understanding their experiences and emotions, and integrating these aspects into your adult self. This process can bring about healing, self-discovery, and personal growth.

The concept of the inner child originates from psychology and represents our childlike aspect. It includes the needs, desires, and experiences we had when we were children. Exploring your inner child can help you understand your emotions, responses, and patterns that are rooted in your childhood.

To begin this exploration, try to recall your childhood experiences. Reflect on what brought you joy, what made you sad, and what made you feel safe or afraid. Use old photos, home videos, or childhood possessions to help trigger memories.

Journaling can be a powerful tool in this journey. Writing about your childhood memories and emotions can provide you with insights into your inner child. Try writing a letter to your inner child, expressing understanding, compassion, and love.

Creative expression, such as drawing, painting, or playing music, can also help you connect with your inner child. These activities can help you express emotions that might be difficult to put into words.

Meditation or guided visualizations can be another effective way to explore your inner child. Imagine meeting your inner child, ask them what they need or want, and listen to their responses.

Exploring your inner child can bring up a range of emotions, and that's okay. It's important to approach this exploration with openness, patience, and self-compassion.

While exploring your inner child can be a powerful journey, it can also be challenging, especially if you've experienced trauma or neglect in your childhood. If this is the case, consider seeking support from a therapist or counselor. They can provide guidance and support as you navigate this journey.

Exploring your inner child is a journey of self-discovery, healing, and growth. It's about understanding your past, nurturing your present, and shaping your future. It's a journey towards a more integrated, self-aware, and fulfilled you.

Your inner child is a part of who you are. By acknowledging and nurturing this part of yourself, you can foster a deeper connection with yourself, heal past wounds, and enrich your life with newfound understanding and compassion. It's a journey that can lead to a more authentic, self-aware, and fulfilling life.

Conscious Self-Reparenting: A Practical Guide

Inner children seek nurturance, acceptance, and guidance. As an adult, you can act as a loving parent for that part of yourself through conscious self-reparenting. Follow these steps to start:

Observe negative beliefs and thoughts. Ask yourself what narratives formed during childhood still influence your view of yourself. Do you have "tapes" in your head criticizing your worth, abilities, or value? Identify harmful self-talk you internalized from past caregivers.

Acknowledge your inner child's needs. Remember that young parts of yourself only want love, safety, and reassurance. Imagine holding the hand of that child and identifying emotions they feel - fear, sadness, longing. Visualize embracing that vulnerable aspect of your being and expressing care.

Replace harsh criticism with compassion. Instead of harsh inner dialogue, practice using kinder self-talk. Move from "I never do things right" to "I'm doing the best I can." Replace "What's wrong with me?" with "I love and accept myself exactly as I am." Even small changes can start breaking negative patterns.

Set appropriate limits. Just as good parents set limits, you must establish boundaries with inner child impulses. Forgive but don't indulge immature desires that don't serve your highest good, such as overspending or making unhealthy choices.

Provide structure and consistency. Reliable routines reduce a child's anxiety. Consider using meditation, journaling, or positive affirmations at the same time each day to nourish your inner child. Build rituals into your schedule that prompt loving self-care and reflection.

Foster curiosity and creativity. Children need outlets for self-expression. Try painting, dancing, playing an instrument, or cooking as therapeutic ways to re-engage your imaginative, playful nature. Nurture a sense of wonder at the world to reawaken joy.

Face challenges with inner strength. When difficult situations arise, recall your resiliency. Tell yourself, "I faced challenges before and prevailed. I can get through this with self-compassion and a determination to grow." Embracing hardship from a place of self-love builds emotional maturity.

Fixing childhood wounds takes time. Begin by simply being kinder to yourself. Treating your inner child with empathy, listening to needs rather than criticism, and acting as a wise, loving parent figure can heal deep hurts and cultivate self-trust from within. Conscious self-reparenting is a lifelong journey of self-discovery and compassion.

Releasing Emotional Blocks and Healing the Inner Child

In the depths of our subconscious lies the wounded inner child, carrying the weight of past experiences and emotional pain. Releasing these emotional blocks and healing the inner child is a vital step in our journey of self-discovery and personal growth. By acknowledging and addressing these wounds with compassion and understanding, we can unlock profound healing and transform our lives.

Understanding Emotional Blocks

Emotional blocks are deeply rooted patterns of thought, emotion, and behavior that stem from unresolved childhood experiences. These blocks can manifest as fear, self-doubt, guilt, shame, or even self-sabotaging behaviors. They act as barriers, preventing us from fully embracing our authentic selves and living fulfilling lives. Recognizing the presence of these emotional blocks is the first step towards healing and growth.

Connecting with the Inner Child

The inner child represents the vulnerable, innocent, and authentic part of ourselves that experienced pain and trauma during childhood. To release emotional blocks, we must establish a compassionate connection with our inner child. This involves creating a safe and nurturing space within ourselves where the inner child feels seen, heard, and acknowledged. By cultivating this connection, we can begin the process of healing and transformation.

Acknowledging and Validating Emotions

One of the fundamental aspects of healing the inner child is acknowledging and validating the emotions that arise from past wounds. It is important to create an environment of non-judgment and acceptance, allowing ourselves to fully experience and express these emotions. By giving ourselves permission to feel, we provide an opportunity for emotional release and healing.

Inner Child Healing Techniques

Various techniques can aid in releasing emotional blocks and healing the inner child. Here are some practical and actionable steps you can take:

- Inner Child Dialogue: Engage in a dialogue with your inner child through journaling or visualization exercises. Listen to their needs, fears, and desires, offering comfort, reassurance, and guidance.
- Inner Child Reparenting: Become the nurturing parent figure your inner child may have lacked. Provide the love, support, and care they needed but may not have received. This process involves practicing self-compassion and self-care.
- Emotional Release: Explore cathartic practices such as art therapy, breathwork, or somatic healing to release pent-up emotions stored within the body. Allow these emotions to surface, be expressed, and gradually let go.

- Forgiveness and Compassion: Extend forgiveness and compassion towards yourself and those who may have caused you pain in the past. This forgiveness frees you from the burden of carrying resentment and allows for emotional healing.

Integrating the Inner Child

Healing the inner child involves integration rather than suppression. As you release emotional blocks and nurture your inner child, you create an opportunity for integration with your present self. Embrace the qualities of joy, playfulness, and spontaneity that the inner child embodies, allowing them to enrich your life and relationships.

The Journey of Healing

Releasing emotional blocks and healing the inner child is a gradual and ongoing process. It requires patience, self-compassion, and a commitment to self-discovery. As you embark on this journey, remember to seek support from trusted individuals, such as therapists or support groups, who can provide guidance and encouragement along the way.

By releasing emotional blocks and healing the inner child, you open yourself up to a life of greater authenticity, self-love, and emotional freedom. Embrace this transformative journey with an open heart and a willingness to explore the depths of your being. You deserve the healing and liberation that awaits you.

Healing the inner child is a chapter of your life story, and with each chapter, you grow closer to embracing your authentic self and living a life aligned with your true purpose.

CHAPTER 5

EMBRACING YOUR AUTHENTIC SELF

Breaking Free from Negative Patterns

The process of breaking free from negative patterns is akin to untangling a complex knot. It requires patience, understanding, and a commitment to personal growth. These patterns can be deeply ingrained through years of repetition and can influence our thoughts, emotions, and behaviors in ways that may not serve our well-being or potential.

Negative patterns often stem from unprocessed emotions, limiting beliefs, or learned behaviors. Identifying these patterns is the first step towards breaking them. This might involve observing your reactions, exploring your feelings, or noticing recurring themes in your thoughts or behaviors.

Once you've identified a negative pattern, seek to understand its origin and purpose. What emotions, beliefs, or experiences might be fueling this pattern? How is this pattern serving you, even if it's in a negative way? Understanding the 'why' behind the pattern can provide valuable insights into how to change it.

Next, challenge the pattern. Question whether it's based on current reality or past experiences. Ask yourself whether it serves your growth, happiness, or well-being. This can help you shift your perspective and open up to the possibility of change.

Replacing a negative pattern with a positive one is the next step. For instance, if you often find yourself dwelling on negative thoughts, you might cultivate a practice of gratitude or positive affirmations. If you tend to isolate yourself when you're stressed, you might reach out to a supportive friend or engage in a relaxing activity.

Changing patterns is a process and it takes time and practice. Be patient with yourself, celebrate your progress, and remember that setbacks are a normal part of the journey.

Seeking support can be beneficial in breaking free from negative patterns. A therapist or coach can provide guidance, encouragement, and strategies to help you navigate this process.

Breaking free from negative patterns is a journey of self-liberation. It's about untangling the knots of past experiences, emotions, and beliefs that have held you back, and weaving a new narrative of empowerment, growth, and well-being.

Remember, breaking free from negative patterns isn't just about eliminating the negatives; it's about creating space for positive growth and change. It's about releasing the old that no longer serves you and embracing new ways of thinking, feeling, and being that align with your highest potential. It's a journey of transformation, empowerment, and self-discovery, leading to a more fulfilled, authentic, and joyful life.

Building Authentic Relationships

Connecting authentically with others starts with honesty within yourself. Use this shadow work workbook to build healthier relationships:

List feelings or experiences you avoid. Do you shy away from emotions like sadness, anger or fear? Note experiences that cause shame or discomfort. Facing these uncomfortable parts of yourself is key to authenticity.

Recall past hurts. Write in depth about emotional injuries from childhood or past relationships. Focus on your reactions and how events still impact you. Forgive yourself for any pain caused while giving that hurting part of you comfort.

Describe your strengths and weaknesses. Make an unfiltered list of your positive and negative traits. Note aspects you want to improve or embrace more fully. Accepting all parts of yourself with compassion opens you up to others.

Identify triggers. Keep a journal for a week, recording any negative reactions to events or people. Look for patterns in what pushes your buttons.Triggers reveal vulnerabilities to address with self-kindness first.

Practice active listening. Make a conscious effort to hear others without judgment. Keep body language open, maintain eye contact and repeat back what they say to ensure understanding. Focus on their perspectives and feelings. This builds trust.

Be honest but kind. When speaking your truth, soften delivery by acknowledging other viewpoints and using "I" statements. Express your authentic self while showing respect and care for others. Connection requires emotional safety for all.

Reframe negative narratives. Replace negative self-talk with positive or neutral statements about yourself and others. Rather than "They don't understand me," try "We have different perspectives." Changing inner dialogue helps form healthier connections.

Acknowledge your limits. Note what you currently cannot offer others and be upfront about boundaries. Saying "I cannot give advice right now but am here to listen" models authenticity and self-care.

Relationships based on honesty about doubts and difficulties ultimately grow the strongest. A shadow work journal prompts reflection that cultivates empathy, self-acceptance and emotional availability - foundations for true intimacy. Authentic connections form when you meet yourself and others where you both truly are.

Instead of trying to be what others want or expect, focus on expressing your whole self with compassion. This transforms relationships from the inside out.

Realigning with Your Authentic Self

The journey to realigning with your authentic self is a transformative path of self-discovery and personal growth. It involves peeling back layers of social conditioning, expectations, and self-imposed limitations to reconnect with your true essence.

The concept of the authentic self refers to who you truly are at your core, beyond societal expectations, roles, and masks. It encompasses your values, passions, talents, and innate wisdom. Reconnecting with your authentic self can bring about a sense of fulfillment, freedom, and alignment in life.

Begin this journey by exploring what authenticity means to you. Reflect on what values are most important to you, what activities make you feel most alive, and when you feel most like 'yourself.' These insights can guide you towards your authentic self.

Another powerful way to reconnect with your authentic self is through self-expression. This could involve expressing your thoughts, feelings, and creativity through art, writing, music, or conversation. Allow your authentic voice to emerge unedited and uncensored.

Practicing mindfulness can also facilitate this reconnection. Mindfulness involves being present and aware of your thoughts, feelings, and experiences without judgment. This can help you tune into your inner voice and intuition, key guides to your authentic self.

It's important to create a safe space for your authentic self to emerge. This might involve setting boundaries, cultivating self-compassion, and surrounding yourself with supportive and accepting people.

Realigning with your authentic self is a journey, not a destination. It requires patience, courage, and self-compassion. Celebrate your progress and remember that each step, no matter how small, brings you closer to your authentic self.

Realigning with your authentic self is a journey of self-discovery, self-acceptance, and self-expression. It's about shedding the masks, embracing your uniqueness, and living in alignment with your true essence.

Your authentic self is your most natural state of being. By realigning with this self, you're not becoming someone new, but coming home to who you've always been. It's a journey of shedding layers, revealing your truth, and embracing your inherent worthiness. It's a journey that can lead to a more fulfilled, joyful, and authentic life.

Living Your Life Purpose: A Step-by-Step Guide

Unveiling and living your life purpose is a transformative journey, akin to a treasure hunt. It involves deep self-exploration, courage to face the unknown, and commitment to align your life with your deepest truths. This step-by-step guide will illuminate the path towards living your life purpose.

The concept of life purpose refers to a central goal or theme that gives your life meaning, direction, and fulfillment. It's unique for each person and can be related to career, relationships, personal growth, service, or creative expression.

The first step towards living your life purpose is to explore what truly matters to you. Reflect on your values, passions, talents, and the experiences or themes that have been significant in your life. You might find it helpful to journal, meditate, or engage in creative activities to deepen this exploration.

Next, envision how your life would look if it were fully aligned with these elements. What would you be doing? Who would you be with? How would you feel? This vision can provide a beacon towards your life purpose.

Once you've identified your life purpose, start aligning your life with it. This could involve setting goals, making changes in your career or lifestyle, or pursuing new learning or experiences. Remember, this alignment is a process, not a one-time event.

It's important to cultivate a mindset of openness, courage, and resilience. You'll likely face challenges, doubts, and fears along this journey. See these not as obstacles, but as opportunities for growth and learning.

Make sure to regularly check in with yourself and reflect on your progress. Are your actions and decisions aligning with your life purpose? What challenges are you facing? What have you learned? This reflection can provide valuable insights and keep you on track.

Living your life purpose is a journey of self-discovery, courage, and transformation. It's about aligning with your deepest truths, expressing your unique gifts, and creating a life that feels meaningful and fulfilling.

Remember, your life purpose is not a fixed destination, but a direction. It's a compass guiding you towards a life of authenticity, fulfillment, and growth. By living your life purpose, you're not only contributing to your own joy and fulfillment, but also to the well-being of others and the world. It's a journey that brings the best of who you are into the world, and in turn, makes the world a better place.

CHAPTER 6

CULTIVATING SELF-COMPASSION

Understanding Self-Compassion: Definition and Importance

Embarking on the journey to understand self-compassion is akin to learning a new language—the language of kindness towards oneself. This language, once embraced, has the power to transform our relationship with ourselves and our experiences, fostering a sense of inner peace, resilience, and well-being.

Self-compassion, as defined by psychologist Dr. Kristin Neff, involves treating ourselves with the same kindness, understanding, and patience that we would offer to a dear friend. It's about acknowledging our imperfections, accepting our vulnerabilities, and extending grace to ourselves, especially in moments of struggle or failure.

The importance of self-compassion lies in its capacity to alleviate self-criticism, guilt, and perfectionism, common tendencies that can lead to stress, anxiety, and depression. By adopting a self-compassionate mindset, we allow ourselves to make mistakes, learn from them, and continue our journey of growth and self-improvement.

Understanding self-compassion requires us to recognize that suffering and imperfection are part of the shared human experience. We all face challenges and make mistakes. Instead of isolating ourselves in these moments, self-compassion encourages us to connect with the collective human experience of imperfection.

Self-compassion also involves mindfulness, which is the ability to observe our experiences neutrally, without judgment or suppression. Through mindfulness, we learn to acknowledge our feelings and thoughts, including negative ones, without identifying with them or allowing them to consume us.

Cultivating self-compassion doesn't mean ignoring or avoiding personal responsibility. It's about acknowledging our missteps, without harsh judgment, and considering what we can learn or how we can grow from these experiences.

Self-compassion is a powerful ally in the journey of personal growth and mental well-being. It's a gentle, understanding friend that encourages us to learn, grow, and heal, instead of a harsh critic that pulls us down.

Remember, self-compassion isn't a trait that we either have or don't have. It's a skill that can be cultivated and strengthened over time. With practice, patience, and perseverance, we can all learn to speak the language of self-compassion. And in doing so, we not only enhance our relationship with ourselves but also our ability to navigate life's challenges with resilience, grace, and inner peace.

The Three Elements of Self-Compassion

Sailing on the sea of self-compassion, you'll come across three key islands that form the archipelago of self-kindness: self-kindness, common humanity, and mindfulness. These three elements, identified by Dr. Kristin Neff, are the pillars that uphold the practice of self-compassion.

Self-kindness, the first pillar, involves being gentle, supportive, and understanding towards ourselves, especially during times of struggle or failure. It's about replacing self-criticism with self-encouragement, and self-judgment with self-acceptance. Practicing self-kindness may involve positive self-talk, self-care activities, or simply giving ourselves permission to rest and recharge.

The second pillar, common humanity, recognizes that suffering, imperfection, and failure are part of the shared human experience. We all face challenges, make mistakes, and experience disappointments. Remembering this can help us feel connected rather than isolated during difficult times. It's about acknowledging that we're not alone in our struggles, which fosters a sense of belonging and interconnectedness.

Mindfulness, the third pillar, is the ability to observe our feelings and thoughts without judgment or avoidance. It involves being present with our experiences, whether they're pleasant or unpleasant, and acknowledging them with openness and curiosity. Mindfulness allows us to witness our suffering without becoming overwhelmed by it, providing us with the space to respond with self-compassion.

Practicing these three elements of self-compassion can be transformative. It can alleviate stress, foster resilience, and enhance our overall well-being. It's like learning a new language— the language of self-love and self-acceptance.

Like any skill, self-compassion takes time and practice to cultivate. Be patient with yourself, celebrate your progress, and remember that each moment of self-compassion is a step towards greater self-understanding, self-acceptance, and inner peace.

Self-compassion isn't about ignoring our faults or avoiding responsibility. It's about recognizing our imperfections, acknowledging our shared humanity, and mindfully navigating our experiences with kindness and understanding. By cultivating these three elements, we can transform our relationship with ourselves, enhancing our resilience, emotional well-being, and capacity for personal growth. It's a journey that leads us to a more compassionate, accepting, and loving relationship with ourselves.

The Role of Mindfulness in Self-Compassion

As a river irrigates and nourishes the land, mindfulness irrigates and nourishes the soil of self-compassion. It is the bedrock upon which self-compassion flourishes, providing the awareness and presence necessary to respond to ourselves with kindness and understanding.

Mindfulness, at its core, is the practice of being fully present and engaged in the current moment, observing our thoughts, feelings, and experiences without judgment or avoidance. It's about creating a compassionate space for our experiences, rather than suppressing them or getting swept away by them.

In the context of self-compassion, mindfulness serves several key roles. Firstly, it helps us recognize when we're suffering. Often, we might be so caught up in our struggles that we don't even acknowledge our pain. Mindfulness brings our attention to our suffering, the first step towards responding with self-compassion.

Secondly, mindfulness allows us to observe our thoughts and feelings without judgment. It helps us see our self-critical thoughts as what they truly are—just thoughts, not facts. This perspective can reduce the power of self-critical thoughts and open the door to self-kindness.

Thirdly, mindfulness helps us manage difficult emotions with balance. Instead of becoming overwhelmed by our pain or trying to avoid it, mindfulness encourages us to sit with our feelings, acknowledging them with kindness and patience. This mindful approach to difficult emotions is a core aspect of self-compassion.

Mindfulness, however, is not a destination, but a journey. It's a skill that requires consistent practice. Mindfulness exercises, meditation, yoga, or simply taking a few moments each day to tune into your senses can help cultivate mindfulness.

Mindfulness is not about emptying our minds or achieving a state of eternal calm. It's about becoming aware of our experiences and meeting them with curiosity, openness, and compassion. It's about being fully present in the here and now, and greeting ourselves with kindness and understanding.

Remember, mindfulness is not just a tool for personal growth or stress reduction—it's a way of life. By incorporating mindfulness into our daily lives, we not only cultivate self-compassion, but also enhance our overall well-being, resilience, and joy. It's a journey that leads us to a deeper connection with ourselves, others, and the world around us, fostering a sense of peace, clarity, and compassion in our lives.

Practices to Cultivate Self-Compassion

Cultivating self-compassion is much like tending to a garden. It requires consistent care, patience, and the right tools. Fortunately, there are several practical practices that can help nurture the seeds of self-compassion, allowing it to take root and blossom within us.

One effective practice is mindfulness meditation, specifically loving-kindness and self-compassion meditations. These practices involve silently repeating phrases of kindness and compassion towards oneself, fostering a mindset of self-love and acceptance.

Another powerful practice is journaling. Writing about your experiences, emotions, and thoughts can provide a safe space to express your feelings and extend compassion to yourself. It allows you to witness your own suffering, acknowledge it, and respond to it with kindness.

The practice of self-compassion also involves consciously shifting our self-talk. When you notice self-critical thoughts, try to reframe them with kindness and understanding. Instead of harshly judging yourself for a mistake, remind yourself that everyone makes mistakes and they're opportunities for learning and growth.

Engaging in self-care activities is another way to practice self-compassion. These activities can range from taking a relaxing bath, going for a walk in nature, practicing yoga, or simply taking a few moments to breathe deeply and mindfully. These acts of self-care are expressions of self-compassion, signaling to ourselves that we are worthy of care and kindness.

Cultivating self-compassion is a journey, not a destination. It takes time, practice, and patience. There might be times when self-criticism takes the upper hand, and that's okay. The key is to notice these moments and gently guide your attention back to compassion and understanding.

Remember, self-compassion is a skill, and like any skill, it flourishes with practice. Even small moments of self-compassion can create a ripple effect, gradually transforming your relationship with yourself. By integrating these practices into your daily life, you're not only nurturing self-compassion, but also sowing the seeds for greater peace, resilience, and joy. It's a journey that illuminates the path to a kinder, more compassionate relationship with yourself.

Benefits of Self-Compassion in Personal Growth

Just as sunlight nurtures the growth of plants, self-compassion fosters personal growth. It illuminates the path to self-understanding, self-acceptance, and self-improvement, fostering a resilient and growth-oriented mindset.

One of the key benefits of self-compassion is that it promotes mental well-being. Research has shown that self-compassion is associated with lower levels of stress, anxiety, and depression. By treating ourselves with kindness and understanding, we can navigate life's challenges more effectively and maintain emotional balance.

Self-compassion also fosters resilience, the ability to bounce back from adversity. When we approach our struggles with self-compassion, we acknowledge our pain without becoming overwhelmed by it. This makes it easier to recover from setbacks and continue our journey of personal growth.

By cultivating self-compassion, we can also enhance our self-esteem. Instead of basing our worth on external achievements or the approval of others, self-compassion encourages us to value ourselves for who we are. This fosters a more stable and authentic sense of self-worth.

Furthermore, self-compassion supports healthy relationships. When we're compassionate towards ourselves, it becomes easier to extend compassion to others. This can improve our relationships with family, friends, colleagues, and even strangers.

Self-compassion can also boost our motivation for personal growth. Instead of being driven by fear of failure or harsh self-criticism, we're motivated by a desire for self-improvement and well-being. This makes the process of personal growth more enjoyable and sustainable.

Self-compassion isn't a luxury—it's a necessity. It's a key ingredient for personal growth and mental well-being. By treating ourselves with kindness, understanding, and patience, we not only alleviate our suffering but also create the space for growth, transformation, and fulfillment.

The benefits of self-compassion extend beyond the realm of personal growth. Cultivating self-compassion can also enhance our overall quality of life, fostering a sense of peace, joy, and fulfillment. It's a practice that not only benefits ourselves but also the people around us. As we become gentler with ourselves, we naturally become gentler with others, contributing to a more compassionate and understanding world.

CHAPTER 7

EMBRACING VULNERABILITY

Vulnerability: Redefining Strength and Courage

Venturing into the realm of vulnerability is like stepping into a new landscape, one where strength and courage take on new definitions. In this landscape, strength is not about invulnerability, but the courage to show up, be seen, and live authentically, even when it feels risky or uncomfortable.

Vulnerability, as defined by research professor Dr. Brené Brown, is the emotion that we experience during times of uncertainty, risk, and emotional exposure. It's about being open and authentic, even when it means revealing parts of ourselves that are messy, imperfect, or susceptible to judgment or hurt.

Redefining strength and courage involves recognizing vulnerability as a source of power, rather than weakness. When we allow ourselves to be vulnerable, we demonstrate the courage to be ourselves, to express our feelings, and to connect authentically with others. This vulnerability is a testament to our strength and resilience.

Vulnerability also paves the way for greater self-awareness and self-acceptance. By acknowledging and expressing our vulnerabilities, we become more in tune with our authentic selves. This self-awareness is a necessary step towards self-growth and self-improvement.

Moreover, vulnerability fosters deeper connections with others. By revealing our authentic selves, we invite others to do the same. This mutual openness can lead to more meaningful and fulfilling relationships.

Embracing vulnerability can also enhance our capacity for empathy and compassion, both towards ourselves and others. When we acknowledge our own vulnerabilities, we're more likely to respond with kindness and understanding when we see vulnerability in others.

Vulnerability is not about oversharing or disregarding boundaries. It's about being courageous enough to express our true feelings and experiences, in contexts where it feels safe and appropriate to do so.

Remember, vulnerability is a journey, not a destination. It's a continuous process of opening ourselves up, embracing our authentic selves, and connecting deeply with others. By redefining strength and courage through the lens of vulnerability, we not only foster personal growth, but also contribute to a more authentic, compassionate, and connected world. It's a journey that leads us to greater self-understanding, deeper connections, and a more authentic and fulfilling life.

The Fear of Vulnerability: Risks and Rewards

The fear of vulnerability often feels like standing on the edge of a cliff, the wind of uncertainty whipping around, the depths of potential rejection and disappointment looming below. This fear, while universal, can be limiting, preventing us from living authentically and forming deep connections.

Fear of vulnerability often stems from past experiences of hurt, rejection, or criticism. It's a protective mechanism designed to shield us from potential pain. However, while this fear might protect us from negative experiences, it can also block us from positive ones—deep connections, authentic living, and personal growth.

The risks of vulnerability are real. Opening ourselves up can lead to rejection, criticism, or misunderstanding. However, avoiding vulnerability also comes with risks. It can lead to feelings of isolation, inauthenticity, and unfulfillment. It can prevent us from forming deep, meaningful relationships and living in alignment with our true selves.

The rewards of vulnerability, on the other hand, are profound. Vulnerability allows us to live authentically, embracing our true selves with all our strengths and flaws. It fosters deeper connections with others, as vulnerability invites authenticity and understanding.

Vulnerability can also lead to personal growth. When we allow ourselves to be vulnerable, we step out of our comfort zones. This can lead to new experiences, insights, and personal development.

To navigate the fear of vulnerability, it can be helpful to start small. Choose safe, supportive environments to express your vulnerability. Practice self-compassion, acknowledging your fear and responding with kindness and understanding.

The fear of vulnerability is a common human experience. It's okay to feel scared, and it's okay to take your time. Embracing vulnerability is a journey, not a destination.

Remember, vulnerability is not a sign of weakness but a testament to courage. The fear of vulnerability is just another part of the human experience, and navigating this fear is a journey towards authenticity, connection, and personal growth. By acknowledging the risks and rewards of vulnerability, we can make informed decisions about when and how to express our vulnerability, fostering a more authentic and fulfilling life.

Vulnerability and Authenticity

Navigating the paths of vulnerability and authenticity is like traversing a forest, where each tree represents a different aspect of ourselves. Some trees are tall and strong, symbolizing our strengths and achievements. Others might be bent or have broken branches, symbolizing our flaws and failures. Authenticity involves acknowledging and embracing this entire forest, not just the tall and strong trees.

Vulnerability is the gateway to authenticity. It involves revealing our true selves—our thoughts, feelings, experiences, and beliefs— even when it feels risky or uncomfortable. It's about removing our masks and showing up as we truly are.

Authenticity, on the other hand, is the practice of acknowledging and expressing our true selves. It's about aligning our actions with our values, beliefs, and feelings. Authenticity fosters a sense of integrity, self-respect, and self-acceptance.

Vulnerability and authenticity are intertwined. Vulnerability allows us to access and express our authentic selves, while authenticity encourages us to be vulnerable, to show up without masks or pretenses.

Embracing vulnerability and authenticity can enhance our relationships, as it invites deeper understanding and connection. It can also foster personal growth, as it provides the space for self-understanding, self-acceptance, and self-improvement.

However, vulnerability and authenticity can also feel risky. They expose us to potential judgment, rejection, or misunderstanding. It's important to choose safe, supportive environments to express our vulnerability and authenticity.

Vulnerability and authenticity are not one-time events, but ongoing practices. They require courage, self-compassion, and resilience.

Remember, vulnerability and authenticity are not signs of weakness, but indications of courage and strength. By embracing these practices, we honor our true selves, foster deeper connections, and pave the way for personal growth. It's a journey that leads us towards a more fulfilling, authentic, and compassionate life.

Practical Steps to Embrace Vulnerability

Embracing vulnerability is akin to embarking on a courageous journey, a journey that requires courage, self-awareness, and resilience. Here are some practical steps that can guide you along this path.

The first step on this journey is acknowledging your fear of vulnerability. It's okay to feel scared or uncomfortable about opening up—it's a natural human response. Practice self-compassion and remind yourself that it's okay to feel this way.

Next, identify safe spaces and supportive people where you can express your vulnerability. These could be trusted friends, family members, therapists, or support groups. Remember, vulnerability is about sharing our true selves with others, so it's important to choose environments where we feel seen, heard, and respected.

Another crucial step is practicing mindfulness. Mindfulness can help you tune into your feelings and experiences, fostering greater self-awareness. This awareness can make it easier to identify and express your vulnerabilities.

It's also important to set and respect your own boundaries. Vulnerability is not about oversharing or ignoring your comfort levels. It's about expressing your authentic self in a way that feels right for you.

Journaling is another effective tool for embracing vulnerability. Writing about your thoughts, feelings, and experiences can provide a safe, private space to explore your vulnerabilities.

Be patient with yourself. Embracing vulnerability is a journey, not a destination. It takes time, practice, and lots of self-compassion.

Vulnerability is not a sign of weakness, but a testament to your strength and courage. Each step you take towards embracing vulnerability is a step towards greater authenticity, connection, and personal growth.

Remember, vulnerability is a gift that we give to ourselves and others. By embracing vulnerability, we not only foster our own personal growth and self-acceptance, but also contribute to a more authentic, compassionate, and connected world. It's a journey that opens up new possibilities for connection, authenticity, and personal fulfillment.

The Role of Vulnerability in Building Deep Connections

Imagine vulnerability as a bridge, a structure that connects two sides. In the realm of human connections, vulnerability serves as that bridge, allowing us to cross over from superficial interactions to deeper, more meaningful relationships.

Vulnerability plays a crucial role in building deep connections. It involves revealing our authentic selves—our thoughts, feelings, experiences, and beliefs—even when it feels risky or uncomfortable. This openness invites authenticity, understanding, and empathy, fostering deeper connections.

When we express vulnerability, we show others that we are human, with our own strengths and weaknesses, successes and failures, joys and sorrows. This authenticity can inspire others to lower their own defenses, fostering mutual openness and understanding.

Vulnerability can also enhance empathy, the ability to understand and share the feelings of others. When we express our vulnerabilities, we give others a glimpse into our inner world. This can foster empathy, as others can relate to our experiences on a human level.

Moreover, vulnerability fosters trust, a key ingredient for deep connections. When we share our vulnerabilities, we show others that we trust them with our authentic selves. This trust can strengthen the bond between us, paving the way for deeper connections.

Practicing vulnerability, however, requires courage, self-compassion, and discernment. It's important to choose safe, supportive environments to express our vulnerability. It's also crucial to respect our own boundaries and comfort levels.

Vulnerability is not a sign of weakness, but a testament to our strength and courage. It's the bridge that leads us from superficial interactions to deep, meaningful connections.

The power of vulnerability extends beyond our personal lives. By embracing vulnerability, we contribute to a more authentic, compassionate, and connected world. It's a journey that not only enriches our relationships but also fosters a greater sense of understanding, empathy, and shared humanity. It's a journey that illuminates the path to deeper connections, greater understanding, and a more compassionate world.

CHAPTER 8

28 DAYS PLAN

This plan is designed to take less than 15 minutes each day, providing you with a focused reflection for 28 days. It offers a quick exercise for those who prefer a shorter practice or the option to spend more time for a deeper exploration. Remember to find a quiet space to engage in these exercises and set a timer if you have time constraints or commitments after.

Day 1: Introduction to Shadow Work

Read the introduction to the book and set your intentions for the 28-day journey.

Reflect on your expectations and write down what you hope to gain from this process.

Day 2: Defining Your Shadows

Spend time journaling about your understanding of shadow work.

Identify and write down three aspects of yourself that you consider to be "shadows."

Day 3: Exploring Emotional Triggers

Identify three situations or experiences that consistently trigger strong emotional responses in you.

Reflect on the underlying emotions and patterns associated with these triggers.

Day 4: Belief Assessment

Write down five beliefs you hold about yourself that limit your personal growth.

Challenge each belief by finding evidence to the contrary and write down a more empowering belief.

Day 5: Mirror Technique

Stand in front of a mirror and observe your reflection.

Talk to yourself as if you were speaking to your inner child, offering love, acceptance, and encouragement.

Day 6: Inner Child Visualization

Find a quiet space, close your eyes, and visualize yourself as a child.

Spend time connecting with your inner child and offer them love, comfort, and reassurance.

Day 7: Healing Visualization

Visualize a healing light surrounding your inner child, bringing warmth and healing to any wounds.

Journal about the emotions and sensations that arise during this visualization.

Day 8: Breaking Free from Negative Patterns

Identify one recurring negative pattern or behavior in your life.

Develop a plan of action to interrupt and replace this pattern with a more positive and empowering one.

Day 9: Authentic Self-Expression

Engage in a creative activity that allows you to express your authentic self (e.g., painting, dancing, writing).

Reflect on how it feels to express yourself authentically and without judgment.

Day 10: Mindfulness Meditation

Practice a guided mindfulness meditation, focusing on the present moment and observing your thoughts and emotions without judgment.

Day 11: Self-Compassion Practice

Write yourself a compassionate letter, acknowledging your struggles, offering understanding, and providing words of encouragement.

Day 12: Embracing Vulnerability

Identify one area of your life where you feel the fear of vulnerability.

Take a small step towards embracing vulnerability in that area, whether it's expressing your feelings or asking for support.

Day 13: Reflection and Integration

Review your journal entries from the past 12 days.

Identify any patterns, insights, or shifts in your awareness and write a summary of your reflections.

Day 14: Identifying Triggers

Make a list of situations or experiences that consistently trigger strong emotional responses in you.

Reflect on the underlying emotions and patterns associated with these triggers.

Day 15: Shadow Journal

Set aside time to journal about your shadows and any new insights that have emerged.

Reflect on how these shadows have influenced your thoughts, behaviors, and relationships.

Day 16: Writing Your Shadow Story

Write a short narrative or poem that expresses the essence of one of your shadows.

Explore the emotions and experiences associated with this shadow in your writing.

Day 17: Embracing Light and Dark

Create a visual representation of the integration of light and dark within yourself (e.g., collage, drawing, or painting).

Reflect on the balance between these aspects and how they contribute to your wholeness.

Day 18: Letter to Your Younger Self

Write a compassionate letter to your younger self, offering love, understanding, and guidance.

Express any apologies, forgiveness, or words of encouragement that you feel are necessary.

Day 19: Release through Art

Engage in an artistic activity that allows you to express and release emotions associated with your shadows (e.g., painting, sculpting, or dancing).

Let the creative process be a cathartic and transformative experience.

Day 20: Self-Forgiveness Practice

Reflect on any past mistakes or regrets that have weighed heavily on you.

Write a letter to yourself, forgiving and releasing yourself from these burdens.

Day 21: Gratitude for Shadows

Make a list of the lessons and growth opportunities that have come from your shadows.

Express gratitude for the wisdom and strength you've gained through these experiences.

Day 22: Embodying Your Authentic Self

Engage in a body-based practice, such as yoga, dance, or mindful movement.

Focus on connecting with your body and allowing your authentic self to be expressed through movement.

Day 23: Sacred Space Creation

Set up a dedicated space in your home as a sacred space for reflection, healing, and inner work.

Decorate it with meaningful objects, symbols, or images that inspire and support your shadow work.

Day 24: Connecting with Nature

Spend time in nature, observing and reflecting on the cycles of growth, decay, and transformation.

Notice how nature mirrors the process of shadow work and draw inspiration from it.

Day 25: Affirming Your Wholeness

Create a list of affirmations that emphasize your wholeness and integration of light and shadow.

Repeat these affirmations daily and notice how they shift your perspective and self-perception.

Day 26: Letting Go Ceremony

Perform a symbolic letting go ceremony to release any attachments to past wounds or negative patterns.

This could involve writing down what you wish to let go of and burning or burying it as a symbolic act of release.

Day 27: Integration and Celebration

Review your journal entries and reflections from the past 26 days.

Celebrate your progress and growth by engaging in an activity that brings you joy and fulfillment.

Day 28: Future Commitments

Reflect on how you will continue to integrate shadow work into your life beyond the 28-day journey.

Set specific commitments or intentions for ongoing personal growth and self-discovery.

BONUS 1

7 EXTRA EXERCISES

Emotional Release Through Writing: Heartfelt Letter to Yourself

Take a dedicated period of time to engage in an emotional release exercise by writing a heartfelt letter to yourself. This exercise offers you a safe and therapeutic space to express and release any unresolved emotions, frustrations, or fears that may be weighing you down. The process of writing allows you to explore your innermost thoughts and feelings, providing an outlet for emotional catharsis and self-reflection.

Here's a detailed explanation of the exercise:

- **Prepare Your Space**: Find a quiet and comfortable environment where you can focus without distractions. Set up a space that feels nurturing and safe, ensuring that you have ample time for this exercise.
- **Set an Intention**: Begin by setting an intention for the emotional release exercise. Clarify your purpose for engaging in this process, whether it's to let go of emotional baggage, gain clarity, or promote healing and personal growth.

- **Reflect on Your Emotions**: Take a few moments to close your eyes and tune in to your current emotional state. Notice any unresolved emotions, frustrations, or fears that may be present within you. Identify the specific emotions you wish to address in your letter.

- **Begin Writing**: Open a blank document or grab a pen and paper. Address the letter to yourself, using your own name or endearing term that feels comforting. Start writing without judgment or censorship. Let the emotions flow through your words as you express yourself honestly and authentically. Write as if you were having an open and heartfelt conversation with yourself.

- **Express and Release Emotions**: Allow yourself to freely express the emotions you identified earlier. Share your thoughts, fears, and frustrations openly. Release any pent-up feelings that you may have been holding onto. Let the words flow from your heart, and do not worry about grammar, spelling, or punctuation. This is a personal and cathartic exercise, and it's the emotional release that matters.

- **Reflect and Gain Insights**: Once you have completed your letter, take a moment to read it back to yourself. As you reflect on your words, pay attention to any patterns, insights, or revelations that arise. Consider how the act of writing has allowed you to process and release these emotions.

- **Closure and Self-Compassion**: Conclude the exercise with a sense of closure and self-compassion. Acknowledge the strength it took to explore your emotions and honor your vulnerability. Offer yourself words of comfort, compassion, and support as you move forward on your journey of healing and self-discovery.

- **Journaling or Additional Reflection**: If you feel inclined, you may choose to journal further about the emotions and insights that arose during the exercise. Use this as an opportunity to deepen your self-reflection and gain a clearer understanding of your emotional landscape.

Shadow Exploration Through Dream Analysis: Unveiling Insights from Your Dreams

Engage in the practice of dream analysis as a means to explore your shadow aspects and delve into the depths of your inner self. By keeping a dream journal and taking time to analyze recurring themes, symbols, and emotions in your dreams, you can gain valuable insights that will illuminate the connection between your dreams and your inner exploration.

Here's a detailed explanation of the exercise:

- **Establish a Dream Journal**: Set up a dedicated notebook or use a digital tool to keep track of your dreams. Place it near your bed to ensure easy access upon waking.
- **Commit to Daily Recording**: As soon as you wake up, take a few minutes to jot down your dream(s) in your journal. Include any vivid details, emotions, people, objects, or scenarios that you can recall. Don't worry about writing in perfect prose; simply capture the essence of your dream.
- **Identify Recurring Themes**: Over time, you may notice certain themes, symbols, or scenarios that appear frequently in your dreams. Pay attention to these recurring

elements, as they often hold significant meaning related to your shadow aspects.

- **Explore Emotions and Reactions**: Reflect on the emotions you experienced during the dream and upon waking. Consider how these emotions may be connected to your subconscious thoughts, fears, desires, or unresolved aspects of your psyche.

- **Uncover Symbolism**: Identify any symbols or objects that appeared in your dreams. Analyze their potential meanings and personal associations. Take note of the feelings or memories they evoke and consider how they may relate to your shadow aspects.

- **Connect Dreams to Shadow Work**: Begin drawing connections between your dreams and your shadow aspects. Reflect on how the symbols, emotions, and recurring themes align with specific aspects of your personality that you are exploring through shadow work.

- **Engage in Reflection**: Dedicate regular time for reflection and analysis of your dream journal entries. Look for patterns, shifts, or progress in your dreams over time. Consider the insights gained from the dreams and how they can inform your journey of self-discovery.

Expressive Movement Therapy: Unlocking Emotions Through Free-Form Movement

Engage in the practice of expressive movement therapy, using music as a catalyst to guide your body in free-form movement. By allowing your body to lead the way and expressing emotions through movement, you create a powerful opportunity for emotional release, self-expression, and insight. Pay close attention to the sensations, emotions, and insights that arise during this practice.

Here's a detailed explanation of the exercise:

- **Create a Safe Space**: Find a private space where you can move freely without distractions. Clear the area of any potential obstacles to ensure a safe and open environment for movement.
- **Set the Mood**: Choose music that resonates with your emotions or sets the tone for the specific emotions you wish to explore. Create a playlist or select a single track that evokes the desired mood or energy.
- **Set an Intention**: Before you begin, set an intention for your expressive movement practice. Clarify the emotions or energies you wish to explore, release, or cultivate. Focus on being present and open to whatever arises.
- **Start with Centering**: Take a few moments to stand still, close your eyes, and connect with your body and breath. Ground yourself by feeling the weight of your feet on the ground. Take deep breaths, allowing any tension or distractions to melt away.
- **Let Your Body Lead**: As the music starts playing, let your body be the guide. Release any preconceived notions of how you should move and let go of inhibitions. Allow your body to move spontaneously, without judgment or self-consciousness.
- **Explore Different Movements**: Experiment with various movements—slow, fast, gentle, vigorous. Let your body express emotions, energies, and sensations through its own

unique dance. There are no right or wrong movements; simply let your body freely express itself.

- **Pay Attention to Sensations and Emotions**: As you move, pay close attention to the physical sensations in your body and the emotions that arise. Notice any areas of tension or areas that feel alive and energized. Observe how the movements affect your emotional state.

- **Journaling and Reflection**: After your expressive movement session, take time to reflect on your experience. Journal about the emotions, insights, or revelations that surfaced during the practice. Write freely, allowing your thoughts and feelings to flow onto the pages.

- **Integration and Self-Care**: Take care of yourself following the practice. Engage in activities that promote relaxation, self-care, and integration, such as taking a warm bath, journaling further, or engaging in a quiet, calming activity.

- **Regular Practice**: Incorporate regular sessions of expressive movement therapy into your routine. Aim for consistency to allow for deeper exploration and emotional release. The more you engage in this practice, the more insights and benefits you may discover.

Ancestral Healing Ritual: Honoring and Healing Your Ancestral Lineage

Engage in an ancestral healing ritual to honor and heal your ancestral lineage. By researching ancestral healing practices or rituals that resonate with you, creating a sacred space, and offering words or prayers of healing and gratitude to your ancestors, you can reflect on how ancestral patterns and wounds may have influenced your life. Set intentions to break any negative cycles and cultivate healing for yourself and future generations.

Here's a detailed explanation of the exercise:

- **Research Ancestral Healing**: Begin by researching ancestral healing practices or rituals that align with your beliefs and resonate with you personally. Explore various cultural or spiritual traditions, books, online resources, or seek guidance from professionals experienced in ancestral healing.
- **Create a Sacred Space**: Choose a dedicated space where you can conduct your ancestral healing ritual. Clear the area of clutter and distractions. Set up an altar or sacred space that reflects your intentions, incorporating elements such as candles, ancestral photographs, symbolic objects, or items representing your lineage.
- **Set an Intention**: Clarify your intention for the ancestral healing ritual. Reflect on how ancestral patterns and wounds may have influenced your life and the desire to break negative cycles. Focus on healing, gratitude, and cultivating a positive legacy for yourself and future generations.
- **Light Candles**: Begin the ritual by lighting candles on your altar, symbolizing illumination and connection with your ancestors. Take a moment to visualize the warm glow representing their presence and the light they bring to your healing journey.
- **Offer Words or Prayers**: Speak words or offer prayers of healing, gratitude, and connection to your ancestors. Express your intentions, acknowledging the challenges they

faced and the wisdom they passed down. Share your desire to release any burdens or negative patterns carried through generations.

- **Reflect on Ancestral Influence**: Take time to reflect on how ancestral patterns, wounds, and experiences may have impacted your life. Consider both the positive and challenging aspects that have been passed down through generations. Journal about your observations and insights, fostering deeper self-awareness and understanding.

- **Break Negative Cycles**: Set intentions to break any negative cycles or patterns that you have identified. Affirm your commitment to personal healing and growth, offering gratitude to your ancestors for the lessons they have taught you while consciously choosing a different path.

- **Cultivate Healing and Connection**: Spend a few moments in silent contemplation, allowing the energy of healing and connection to permeate your being. Visualize a sense of harmony and unity with your ancestral lineage, knowing that you have the power to create positive change.

- **Express Gratitude**: Express gratitude to your ancestors for their presence, guidance, and the opportunity to heal. Offer thanks for their strength, resilience, and the gifts they have bestowed upon you. Feel a deep sense of appreciation and connection as you honor their legacy.

- **Integration and Continuing Practice**: After the ritual, consider ways to integrate the lessons and healing intentions into your daily life. Explore practices such as journaling, meditation, or engaging in acts of service that honor your ancestral lineage. Continue to nurture your connection with your ancestors, fostering a sense of healing and growth within yourself.

Nature Connection and Elemental Reflection: Finding Inspiration and Grounding in the Elements

Engage in the practice of nature connection and elemental reflection to deepen your understanding of your shadow self. By spending time in nature and connecting with the elements—earth, air, water, and fire—you can reflect on the qualities and energies associated with each element and explore their relationship to different aspects of your shadow. Let the natural environment inspire your inner exploration and provide grounding for your personal growth journey.

Here's a detailed explanation of the exercise:

- **Choose a Natural Setting**: Select a natural setting that resonates with you, such as a forest, park, beach, or garden. Find a quiet and secluded spot where you can connect with the elements without distractions.

- **Set an Intention**: Before immersing yourself in nature, set an intention for your practice. Consider the aspects of your shadow self you wish to explore and how the elements can guide your reflection. Focus on being present and open to the wisdom nature offers.

- **Connect with Earth**: Begin by connecting with the element of Earth. Find a comfortable spot on the ground, preferably on grass, soil, or a rock. Feel the Earth beneath you, supporting and grounding your body. Reflect on the stability, strength, and nurturing qualities associated with Earth, and consider how they relate to your shadow aspects.

- **Engage with Air**: Move to an open area and focus on connecting with the element of Air. Observe the gentle breeze brushing against your skin and flowing through your breath. Reflect on the qualities of clarity, communication, and expansion that Air represents, and explore how they relate to different aspects of your shadow self.

- **Embrace Water**: If possible, find a body of water or a flowing stream. Sit by its side or dip your feet in the water. Allow the element of Water to envelop you. Reflect on the fluidity, emotions, and intuition associated with Water, and contemplate how they connect to your shadow aspects.

- **Witness Fire**: Find a safe space where you can observe the element of Fire. It can be a bonfire, candle flame, or even the warmth of the sun. Gaze at the flames or feel the sun's rays on your skin. Reflect on the transformative, passionate, and illuminating qualities of Fire, considering their relevance to your shadow exploration.

- **Inner Reflection**: As you spend time connecting with each element, reflect on the qualities and energies they embody and how they relate to different aspects of your shadow self. Observe any thoughts, emotions, or insights that arise during this reflection. Allow the elements to inspire your inner exploration and provide a sense of grounding.

- **Gratitude and Integration**: Conclude your nature connection and elemental reflection practice with a moment of gratitude. Offer thanks to the natural environment and the elements for their guidance and inspiration. Consider how you can integrate the lessons and insights gained from this experience into your everyday life and shadow work practice.

Shadow Integration Art Collage: Visualizing the Journey of Embracing and Integrating Shadows

Engage in the practice of creating a shadow integration art collage to visually depict your journey of embracing and integrating your shadows. By collecting images, words, and symbols from magazines or online sources that represent both your shadows and your desired state of integration, you can create a powerful collage that holds deep symbolism and reflection for your personal growth.

Here's a detailed explanation of the exercise:

- **Gather Art Supplies**: Collect the necessary art supplies, including magazines, scissors, glue or tape, a poster board, and any additional materials you may want to use, such as markers, colored pencils, or paint.

- **Set an Intention**: Before beginning the collage, set an intention for the process. Clarify your desire to explore and integrate your shadows, and envision the transformation and growth you seek to achieve through this practice.

- **Collect Images and Words**: Flip through magazines or search online sources for images, words, and symbols that represent both your shadows and your desired state of integration. Look for visuals that resonate with you and evoke the emotions, qualities, or experiences associated with your journey.

- **Create Your Collage**: Start arranging and adhering the collected images, words, and symbols onto the poster board. Allow your creativity to flow as you compose the elements, exploring different layouts and compositions.

There is no right or wrong way to create your collage; let your intuition guide you.

- **Reflect on Symbolism**: Once your collage is complete, take a step back and reflect on the artwork as a whole. Consider the symbolism and messages conveyed by the images, words, and symbols you have chosen. Pay attention to any themes, colors, or patterns that emerge, and contemplate their significance in relation to your personal growth journey.

- **Journaling and Analysis**: Take time to journal about your collage and the insights it brings forth. Write about the specific images, words, and symbols that stand out to you and their representation of your shadows and desired integration. Reflect on how the collage speaks to your inner landscape and the emotions it evokes.

- **Integration and Action**: Consider how the insights gained from your art collage can inform your shadow work practice and your daily life. Explore practical ways to integrate the symbolism and messages into your actions and mindset. Use your collage as a visual reminder of your commitment to embracing and integrating your shadows.

- **Ongoing Reflection**: Display your collage in a place where you can regularly see it. Take moments to revisit the artwork and reflect on the progress you have made in your shadow integration journey. Allow it to serve as a source of inspiration and motivation, reminding you of the transformative potential within you.

Forgiving Others Meditation: Cultivating Empathy, Compassion, and Healing

Engage in the practice of a guided meditation focused on forgiving others who have caused you pain or hardship. This meditation serves as a powerful tool to cultivate empathy, compassion, and release any resentments or negative emotions that may be holding you back from healing and personal growth. By engaging in this practice, you open yourself to the transformative power of forgiveness.

Here's a detailed explanation of the exercise:

- **Find a Suitable Guided Meditation**: Search for a guided meditation specifically focused on forgiveness towards others. Look for meditations that resonate with you and align with your intentions for this practice. You can find such meditations through online platforms, meditation apps, or by working with a qualified meditation teacher or therapist.

- **Create a Calm Environment**: Set up a serene and comfortable space where you can engage in the guided meditation without distractions. Dim the lights, light a candle, or use any other elements that help create a relaxing atmosphere conducive to meditation.

- **Set an Intention**: Before starting the guided meditation, set an intention for your practice. Clarify your desire to cultivate forgiveness, empathy, and compassion towards others who have caused you pain or hardship. Focus on being present and open to the transformative power of forgiveness.

- **Follow the Guidance**: Begin the guided meditation by pressing play or starting the session. Close your eyes, settle into a comfortable position, and allow yourself to relax. Follow the instructions provided by the meditation guide, allowing their words to guide you through the process of forgiveness.

- **Cultivate Empathy and Compassion**: As the meditation progresses, the guide may prompt you to cultivate empathy and compassion towards those who have caused you pain. Visualize their humanity, their own struggles, and their capacity for growth and change. Open your heart to the possibility of understanding their perspective.

- **Release Resentment and Negative Emotions**: The guided meditation may guide you in releasing any resentments or negative emotions you may be holding towards others. Allow yourself to feel the weight of these emotions and consciously choose to release them. Embrace the freedom that forgiveness brings.

- **Self-Forgiveness and Healing**: The meditation may also involve elements of self-forgiveness and self-healing. Embrace the opportunity to extend forgiveness to yourself for any ways in which you may have contributed to the situation. Offer yourself compassion and allow healing to take place within your own heart.

- **Reflection and Integration**: After the guided meditation concludes, take a moment to sit quietly and reflect on your experience. Journal about any insights, emotions, or realizations that emerged during the meditation. Consider how the practice of forgiveness can inform your ongoing healing and personal growth.

- **Continued Practice**: Incorporate forgiveness meditations into your regular practice to deepen your capacity for empathy, compassion, and healing. As you engage in forgiveness towards others, you nurture a space of peace and growth within yourself.

Grover Walton

BONUS 2

AUDIOBOOK

Download the MP3 files by scanning the QR code below and enjoy listening to the audio wherever you go.

AUTHOR BIO

GROVER WALTON

Grover Walton is a renowned author who has dedicated his career to exploring the depths of personal development. With a profound understanding of the human psyche, Grover has become a trusted voice in the field of inner exploration.

Through his captivating writing style and insightful storytelling, he has inspired countless individuals on their paths of self-discovery and healing. With a focus on shadow work, Grover's work delves into the intricate aspects of the human experience, guiding readers to embrace their authentic selves and unlock their true potential.

Through his writings, Grover continues to impact the lives of many, encouraging them to embark on their own journeys of self-reflection and personal growth.

Made in United States
Troutdale, OR
10/05/2023

13406950R00060